AUSTRIA IMPERIAL EDITION

PORTRAIT OF A LIFE

Empress Elisabeth of Austria 1837-1898

The Fate of a Woman Under the Yoke of the Imperial Court

A DOCUMENTATION WITH 130 ILLUSTRATIONS

Renate Hofbauer

FOREWORD

Empress Elisabeth of Austria, 'Sisi' (pronounced 'Sissy') as Emperor Franz Joseph called her, was a legend even during her own lifetime. There are many reasons for this. Not least among these were her fabulous looks coupled with a particular shyness of public appearances. Or the almost exaggerated attention to her own beauty accentuated by a confident refusal to conform to any of the other demands made of her in her role as a woman. Added to this was her natural warmth in dealing with people she valued, but also her frequent and deliberate provocation of Viennese Court society. Her rare presence at official functions, the pains she took to retain her youthfulness and especially her tragic murder, all contributed to the creation of her enigmatic aura, one which continues to fascinate and touch people around the world to this day.

Austria Imperial Edition
Renate Hofbauer
Empress Elisabeth of Austria 1837-1898.
Translation: JLQJ TRANSLATIONS.
Layout: Studio Olschinsky, Vienna.
Production: Lindenau Productions GmbH, Vienna. Printed in Austria - Druckerei Berger, 3580 Horn.
© 1998 by Dr. Renate Hofbauer, Vienna.
ISBN 3-902196-01-7

CONTENTS

A PRINCESS IN BAVARIA

Elisabeth was an exceptional woman in many ways; she led an unusual life and suffered an unusual fate. She was even born on an unusual day, on Christmas Eve 1837. Although whether the tooth she was born with really turned out to be a 'lucky tooth', as it was called at the time, is open to question.

She was one of eight children to Duke Maximilian and Duchess Ludovika in Bavaria. Her childhood was spent in a carefree atmosphere, unmarred by convention and etiquette — her upbringing could almost be described as a 'middle-class' one. Naturally she suffered under the troubled marriage of her parents and dreamt of a life filled with love and happiness for herself. Her mother, Ludovika, became a troubled woman early in life, though, having had to bear the burden and responsibility for the children and the entire ducal household. Her father preferred to enjoy his life in his own way: travelling, indulging in love affairs, engaging in bouts of drinking and the pursuit of his other pastimes such as dressage and hunting. Elisabeth's favourite place to stay was at Posenhofen, their summer palace on Lake Starnberg. There she learned to climb, to fish, to ride, to swim and to cultivate her eye for the beauties of nature. She was never to lose her athletic constitution, nor her love of the outdoors.

It was in this dress that the little princess was christened Elisabeth Amalia Eugenia, just two days after her birth.

Elisabeth's parents Duke Maximilian and Duchess
Ludovika in Bavaria. Ludovika came from the
Bavarian royal family. Through this branch of the
family, Sisi was a second cousin of the future king
of Bavaria, Ludwig II. Ludovika's sister Sophie
was married to Archduke Franz Karl of Austria.
These were Franz Joseph's parents.

Elisabeth was born as the third child of the ducal pair at their winter residence, Max Palace in Munich.

Elisabeth and her family spent the summer months at Possenhofen on Lake Starnberg. She enjoyed happy, untroubled times with her brothers and sisters and other children from the neighbourhood in the midst of the beautiful local countryside.

Duchess Ludovika with the children (from the left) Sophie, Mathilde, Carl Theodor and Max Emanuel. Later Elisabeth was often to escape to the refuge of her own family.

EMPEROR SEEKS EMPRESS

As Archduchess Sophie found that it was high time for her son, the young Emperor Franz Joseph of Austria, to marry she began looking for a suitable bride. Eventually she chose Helene in Bavaria. 'Nene' as she was called, was the eldest daughter of her sister Ludovika. At the time, the younger Elisabeth was only fifteen, in the midst of puberty and lovesick for the first time, as well as having all the other problems associated with her age. To direct her thoughts elsewhere and to remind Franz Joseph's younger brother of her existence, she was permitted to accompany her sister on her journey to the Imperial spa at Bad Ischl for the official betrothal.

Elisabeth's spontaneous naturalness and her honest demeanour worked like magic on the twenty-three year old emperor. He ignored Helene and immediately fell in love with Sisi, as he was to call her later. Two days after their first encounter they were engaged to be married. The young princess was overwhelmed by the course of events. She had fallen head-over-heels in love with her handsome young cousin and doubtless felt very flattered by his advances. 'If only he were a tailor', she sighed, proving that she sincerely loved him for himself and that she saw the rank of Empress as more of a burden than something to be striven for. There was no need to fret over making a decision. 'One does not turn down an emperor', her mother Ludovika told her. And with this, the last word on the matter had been spoken.

Sisi married Franz Joseph for love and had every intention of being a good wife and a faithful companion to him. The following poem, written when her love had long turned to bitterness, shows how happy the couple had initially been (excerpt):

I need not tell you of the time
Which once united us as intimate
And which neither you nor I could ever forget
However endlessly distant it may seem yet.

Do you remember that sweet trice
Where I from will-less frame
Did kiss the soul from thy lips
That it might ever more be mine?

I have perforce, had to battle through
And felt much bitter pain since then;
But to see our love die, though.
Nought hath struck my heart so heavily as that.

*It was love at first sight when the young
Franz Joseph encountered his cousin
Elisabeth.*

Franz Joseph and Elisabeth first met at the spa town of Bad Ischl, and two days later their engagement was announced. Archduchess Sophie gave them the villa they met in as a wedding gift.

*The newly engaged young couple
painted on porcelain.*

Despite being in love, Sisi was plagued by premonitions of her time at Court in Vienna and often looked very serious even before she married the Emperor.

The dress worn by Sisi at the farewell celebrations in Bavaria.

THE WEDDING –
A DREAM OR A NIGHTMARE

After an engagement lasting nine months, Elisabeth left her Bavarian homeland on 20th April 1854. The bridal party travelled to Vienna by ship along the Danube. All along the route people congregated wanting to see the bride, and at every stopping point grand celebrations were held. Three days later their ship docked at Nussdorf near Vienna. Here Elisabeth was awaited by court protocol and a whole series of exhausting official ceremonies.

At last, on 24th April, the wedding was held at the Augustinian Church in Vienna. It was a far from romantic experience for Elisabeth. She was always to remember the exhausting and highly formal celebrations with horror, having been defenceless before the staring masses and being compelled to reveal even the most intimate details of her life to the public. She may have learned 'much and varied' things during her period of engagement — conduct at court, how to make conversation, protocol — but the reality of it all was oppressive to her now. The young bride often broke into tears of despair over the course of these days.

Elisabeth as a sixteen-year old bride.

For the wedding, the Augustinian Church was lit by 15,000 candles and draped in red velvet.

The wedding service began at 7 p.m. on 24th April, 1854. Accompanied by 70 senior members of the clergy the Archbishop of Vienna married Franz Joseph and Elisabeth.

A sketch for Elisabeth's wedding dress. Although we do not know exactly what it looked like, it is certain that it was white. This led to the fashion of marrying in white.

This chasuble is kept in the treasure chamber of the Maria Taferl pilgrimage church in the Wachau; according to tradtion, the embroidery was taken from Sisis wedding dress.

SHADOWS OVER
THE YOUNG MARRIAGE

As a shy young girl, Elisabeth now found herself subjected to perpetual scrutiny and — more than anything — exposed to constant harsh critique. Her lack of experience, the roots of which lay in her upbringing, meant that in the eyes of the court entourage she was no more than a pretty but foolish child. With severity Archduchess Sophie tried to redress what she saw as failings in the young woman's education. Even during their honeymoon at Laxenburg Castle, she inundated her daughter-in-law with commands, rules of conduct and harsh words. Sisi was entirely defenceless against her as Franz Joseph spent his daytime with the business of government at Court in Vienna. Elisabeth was not allowed to choose a lady-in-waiting she could really trust, instead Sophie chose her entire entourage and these had to deliver regular reports of every word uttered by the young Empress. Sophie did not even stop short of prying into Sisi's diaries. She did not understand the accounts of loneliness and homesickness she found in these diaries as a cry for help, but as an unheard-of affront against her son and she reacted with acrimony.

Sisi turned to her husband, the sovereign, for help but he let her down. Sophie was known as 'the only man at Court' and even Franz Joseph opted to take the path of least resistance by demanding that Elisabeth did whatever his mother told her to do. The ability to express his feelings and act according to these had long been drilled out of him in the course of his upbringing. He had not learned anything except how to fulfil his divine calling as a monarch. His surroundings, too, had to conform to any demands this might make. Sisi was driven to despair, even within the first weeks of their marriage.

Archduchess Sophie was both the young Empress Elisabeth's aunt and her mother-in-law.

Sisi spent her honeymoon at the Blue Court of Laxenburg Castle south of Vienna. Most of
the time her mother-in-law and the ladies-in-waiting were her only company.
Archduchess Sophie took the opportunity to begin with the young Empress' education.
Elisabeth bore her sadness to paper in poems. She wrote the following verse fourteen days
after the wedding (excerpt):

Oh, had I but never left the path,
That would have lead to freedom.
Oh, that on the broad avenues
Of vanity I had never strayed!

I have awakened in a dungeon,
With chains on my hands,
And my longing ever stronger —
And freedom. You turned from me!

I have awakened from a rapture,
Which held my spirit captive,
And vainly do I curse this exchange,
In which I gambled away you — Freedom — away

Even on their honeymoon the young Empress only rarely saw her husband, and they actually had very little opportunity for the kind of idyllic stroll shown in this print.

Sisi suffered under hardly being able to spend any time alone with her husband. He always put court protocol and politics first.

In the grand but stifling atmosphere of the royal palace in Vienna, Sisi felt lonely and abandoned.

Schönbrunn Palace, the Imperial summer residence. For Sisi it was just another gilded prison in Vienna.

The couple's shared bedroom at Schönbrunn. The furniture of jacaranda wood was a gift from the Viennese guild of carpenters.

Elisabeth posed only reluctantly. Most of the painters who painted her portrait had to work from memory or using photographs. She made an exception for Franz Schrotzberg. So this picture of the young Empress may be considered to be a reliable account of her true appearance.

When she was
young Elisabeth
liked to wear
white or light
coloured clothes,
in contrast to
later years.

A CHILD DIES

The young Empress gave birth to a girl who was named after Franz Joseph's mother, Sophie, just a year after they were married. In the following year she presented Franz Joseph with another daughter, Gisela. Even though they were both girls, who did not have to be educated for duties as a future monarch, Sisi was not allowed to raise the children herself. She might have given birth to them but she was still too young to bring them up, Sophie decided and took the children away from their mother. Elisabeth later said, 'She took my children from me straight away. I was only allowed to see them when Archduchess Sophie gave her consent. She was always present when I went to visit the children. Eventually I could only concede to her and only seldom went up to see them'. Sisi's pleas to the Emperor to intervene went as good as unheard. It was not until they went away together and were far away from Sophie's influence, that the Emperor at last took his wife's side in the matter and she was able to spend more time with her children again. Then she started openly going against the express wishes of her mother-in-law and even took her little girls with her when she travelled.

The Imperial couple experienced a personal tragedy while on a journey through Hungary: both girls fell ill with diarrhoea and high temperatures. The ten-month old Gisela soon recovered but the two-year old Sophie died in the arms of her mother after a struggle against death which lasted for eleven hours. As if she had not suffered enough, Elisabeth was even indirectly held responsible for the death of her own child. After everything she had been through, Sisi suffered a breakdown. It was all too much for the nineteen-year old Empress. For the first time the physical and psychological symptoms, which were to plague her for the rest of her life in times of crisis, were showing. She completely withdrew for weeks and months at a time, she locked herself in and cried all day. Or she spent hours out riding, keeping going until she reached a state of total exhaustion, just to avoid having to think. Her spiritual and physical health weakened. This was to be seen especially clearly when she even resigned in the battle over her second child. As a result she became emotionally distant towards Gisela and hardly participated at all in her further development. Marie Festetics, an otherwise loyal lady-in-waiting, later commented in her diary that the Empress did not even participate in the preparations for her eldest daughter's wedding. Sisi behaved in a similar way towards her only son, Rudolf, whom she also had to hand over to her mother-in-law as soon as he was born.

The young Imperial couple with their first child, little Sophie (1855–1857).

A poignant detail from an official portrait of the 26-year old Empress: Elisabeth is wearing a likeness of her dead daughter on her arm.

The Emperor and Empress as parents with their daughters Sophie and Gisela.

Sisi with her two-year old Gisela and the new-born Rudolf. A portrait of Sophie, their first daughter who had died a year before, is hanging on the wall.

A picture of Elisabeth and her family...

From the left: Sophie with Gisela, Franz Karl (Franz Joseph's father), Elisabeth, Franz Joseph and little Sophie.

...and a photograph taken just a few years later. From the left, standing: Franz Joseph, his brother Ferdinand Maximilian and his wife Charlotte, the brothers Carl Ludwig and Ludwig Viktor. Seated: Elisabeth with Rudolf and Sophie, between them is Gisela, Franz Karl is to the far right.

Even though Elisabeth often regretted having married when she was so young, she soon began looking for a husband for Gisela. At the age of sixteen she married Prince Leopold of Bavaria. Their marriage, though, was a very happy one and they had four children together.

Daughter Gisela (1856–1932) took after her father and even inherited the same undemanding temperament.

CROWN PRINCE RUDOLF – THE ONLY SON

It was essential that the monarchy had a new heir for the throne. Elisabeth gave birth to such an heir in 1858. He was christened Rudolf. This time she only recovered from the birth slowly and with difficulty. She also had to put this child in the care of her mother-in-law and was never able to build up a real mother-child relationship with him.

Crown Prince Rudolf was an intelligent and very sensitive child. He was also a sickly one and should have been given a great deal of attention. On his sixth birthday he was separated from his beloved sister and Franz Joseph charged Count Gondrecourt with his education. This man had the job of making a 'good soldier' out of Rudolf. To this end, the little crown prince was subjected to relentless and often extremely brutal physical exercises. Some of the consequences of what was supposed to have toughened him up were to trouble him for the rest of his life. Neither anything nor anybody could bring the Emperor to feel any pity for his son. Treatment with water and shocks would have soon reduced him to idiocy, maybe even have cost him his life, as Elisabeth and her lady-in-waiting, Marie Festetics, observed. So Elisabeth intervened, and this time with surprising fervour. She gave the Emperor an ultimatum: Either he left all aspects of the child's upbringing to her or she would leave him. This worked. Gondrecourt was sacked and Rudolf's education was put in the hand of predominantly middle-class, liberal-thinking tutors sought-out by Sisi herself. The deciding factors in making a choice were no longer aristocratic birth or military prowess but purely their academic qualifications. These tutors helped to make a roundly educated, critical and liberal-thinking individual out of Rudolf, just as Elisabeth had hoped they would.

For the rest of his life Rudolf was grateful for his mother's firm-handed intervention. Other than this, though, he hardly really had any kind of a relationship to her at all, just like his sister Gisela. He developed a coy respect and chivalrous admiration for her. He never plucked-up the courage to talk to her about personal matters. For her part, Elisabeth did not really seem to be interested either. So that when he later committed suicide she was also totally unprepared for the shock. She had never even imagined that he was in so much pain (see pages 110-115 for further details).

Crown Prince
Rudolf (1858-1889)
was, if his father
had had his way, to
have become a 'good
soldier', which
means obedient,
fearless and
patriotic. Elisabeth
prevented his being
drilled almost to
death.

Rudolf and his wife, Stephanie of Belgium, encounter Elisabeth and Franz Joseph while strolling in Laxenburg. The marriage between the prince and his princess, which they entered when he was twenty-two and she was sixteen-years old, was an unhappy one for both of them. Following the birth of their first child, christened Elisabeth, Rudolf contracted a venereal disease which he subsequently passed on to his wife, making her incapable of bearing any more children.

Rudolf had inherited his mother's sensitivity and love of freedom and supported the principles of democracy.

IN NEED OF SOLACE

In the first years of their marriage — years in which she was still very vulnerable because of her youth — Sisi had to bear a great deal. That she became increasingly depressed is only too understandable. Then she found out, inevitably, that her husband was cheating on her. This was the last straw. She immediately took Gisela and left Vienna for Possenhofen, to her family. She was now twenty-two years old, had given birth to three children in four years and then lost one of those. She had been badly repaid for all the love and admiration she had shown her husband. She had been extremely lonely in the midst of all the intrigue at Court and found herself caught-up in an endless war of nerves with her mother-in-law. All of this manifested itself in a series of grave problems with her health. Among other symptoms, Elisabeth was already suffering from permanent coughing bouts and there was talk of 'lung trouble'. The difficulty in establishing a clear diagnosis and the lack of success in treatment indicate that the causes were psychosomatic. In any case a cure of several months on Madeira was strongly recommended. Sisi accepted the advice with gratitude as she would have been prepared to do anything to escape the Court in Vienna.

This trip was to mark the beginning of an incessant and restless bout of travelling, which Elisabeth was to embark upon like a refugee for the rest of her life. She was absent from Court in Vienna almost continually for two years. After Madeira, she went on to Corfu, to Venice, to Bad Kissingen and then to Possenhofen. It was during this period that she really began to find an identity of her own.

Not even the formal nature of an official series of photographs can mask Sisi's depressed state-of-mind.

The Emperor inundated his wife with jewellery. However what she sorely missed was his affection and any sense of real security in their marriage.

Here we see some pieces of jewellery made using emeralds originally belonging to Empress Maria Theresia (1740-1780).

Elisabeth's suffering is written all over her face in this photograph. Despite her youth, she bears a striking resemblance to her own mother, who was visibly troubled from a relatively early age.

THE PATH TO ANOREXIA

Sisi's marriage to the Emperor of Austria meant that she was torn abruptly, and unprepared for what was to come, from the security of her surroundings as a very young girl. She was totally lacking in experience of any kind, but for all that she was honest, spontaneous, idealistic and, above all, very shy. Within a few short months she was supposed to become a wife, a mother and the first lady of the Empire at the Imperial Court in Vienna.

Their engagement was announced when she was still in the middle of puberty. The times were such that it is safe to assume she was sent into marriage ignorant of the facts of life. It is unlikely that Franz Joseph, who was already sexually experienced, took this into consideration at all. In any case, their marriage was first consummated in the third night, a source of gossip throughout the palace. Archduchess Sophie made the newly-weds report on their private lives over breakfast, which they had together, also pressing Sisi 'not to spare herself' in the bedroom. After all there had to be an heir to the throne as soon as possible. Sophie also put pressure on the young woman to show herself in public as often as possible during her pregnancy which was, for the times, a most embarrassing thing to do.

The children, and with them a major source of happiness and satisfaction, were taken away from Sisi as soon as they were born. The struggle over their charge was only ended by the death of the little Sophie. Elisabeth tried to gain emotional distance from her second daughter, Gisela (as she later did to her son Rudolf, too), to avoid even more suffering. She suddenly admitted defeat in the tug-o-war over the children's education. The result of all this was that she often felt a yearning for death even when she was still very young.

Added to this was that she was not able to cope with all the intriguing, the gossip, the malicious criticism, the rigorous court ceremony and the perpetual scrutiny. She felt unable to meet the expectations made of her, especially as nobody really helped her to deal with her new station in life.

The worst thing for the despairing young woman was, without doubt, that the man she loved and admired so deeply had no time for her, nor was he really interested, he did not even realise what she was going through. When she got married she believed in true love, and now she was forced to accept that her mother-in-law was the most influential women in her husband's life and that politics and bureaucracy had always been more important to him than she had.

Sisi went about preserving her youthfulness with an obsession. The results were remarkable: at 172cm tall, she never weighed more than 50 kilos and had a waist of 50 to 52cm. This statue in the Hofburg Imperial Palace was made using her actual measurements.

SYMPTOMS OF ANOREXIA

Elisabeth's exaggerated concern with her appearance, her extremely athletic pastimes and her starvation diets were long seen as a sign of her vanity and a lack of fulfilment. Only since the medical profession has begun to take psychosomatic conditions, a close link between the body and one's state-of-mind, seriously has this view broadened. So today we know that there is an illness called *Anorexia nervosa* and that this is caused, like other eating disorders with it, by deep psychological pain. Both the causes and the symptoms can be observed in Elisabeth's case. The causes are to be found in the experiences she made in the early years of marriage.

Among the symptoms of anorexia are problems with one's own female identity, a refusal to eat, exceptional physical restlessness and an obsession with movement as well as a cult-like fixation on one's own appearance. Elisabeth clearly suffered from all of these symptoms.

Any development of a positive attitude to her own female sexuality was obviously stifled from the outset by a range of different experiences. Her experiences with sexuality and with motherly love had both been negative. Her rejection of anything relating to female sexuality reached its peak for Elisabeth later in a general repulsion towards motherhood and little babies, even if these were her own daughters and grandchildren.

She tried to combat her physical restlessness, which left her unable to even sit still for long enough to read or learn anything, with excessive sport. She was one of the best horsewomen of her time, an enthusiastic gymnast, swam, could fence and went for long and arduous hikes regardless of the weather conditions.

She not only stressed her extremely slender figure, the result of not eating and so much sport, with tightly bound corsets but also by having herself literally stitched into her clothes. She cared for her floor-length hair in an exhaustive and time-consuming procedure in which she was prepared to sit for hours at a time to have it arranged in what were veritable artworks. She was also given to bathing in donkey's milk and had a whole range of beauty preparations mixed specially for her by the court apothecary.

Sisi's dressing room at the Hofburg Imperial Palace, which is equipped with gymnastic equipment. She kept fit by exercising here every day.

Elisabeth took her meagre meals in this drawing room at the Hofburg. These often consisted of no more than juice pressed from fresh meat, orange juice or a glass of milk.

One of the magnificent armchairs shown above seen in more detail. It is upholstered in the famous Pineapple Damask, which is still specially produced for Schönbrunn Palace and the Hofburg. It is also used around the world as a wall-covering in many historic buildings. The name stems from the pineapple-like pattern in the weave of this precious cloth. The Pineapple Damask is, and has always been produced by Backhausen in Vienna, cloth-makers by Imperial appointment.

Elisabeth weighed herself three times a day and kept
a tally of her weight in a special book. She liked to
emphasise her narrow waist with flattering belts.

Sisi was dressed and had her hair done in her dressing room (here is the one at Schönbrunn), a process which took several hours every day. She used this time to learn Hungarian and later, to study Greek.

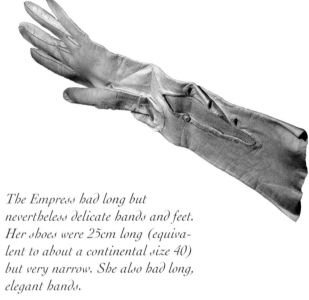

The Empress had long but nevertheless delicate hands and feet. Her shoes were 25cm long (equivalent to about a continental size 40) but very narrow. She also had long, elegant hands.

Her wish for a bathtub caused a scandal at the time but she ignored it. She started each day between 5 and 6 in the morning with a cold bath followed by a massage.

Elisabeth maintained her physical energy and agility into old age. So she was easily able to keep up with the her husband's military stride. Here they are on their last walk together at Bad Kissingen in May 1898.

THE TURNING POINT –
SELF-CONFIDENT AND BEAUTIFUL

Elisabeth reached the full height of her beauty in the eighteen sixties, which means when she was between about twenty-five and thirty-five years old. This was emphasised by the self-confidence she had gained over the years. She was now a mature woman and well aware of the effect she had on others. She enjoyed the admiration she aroused and learned to value the advantages this brought her. She no longer let people tell her what to do and even learned to get her own way. Franz Joseph admired his 'angel' Sisi from a distance without ever really ever knowing her properly as a person.

Elisabeth's beauty became legendary and her public appearances were much-awaited sensations. She did not create her allure with make-up, perfume or any other artificial beauty products, all of which she shunned. Her charm was more the result of a fascinating combination of several natural factors: her height, her svelte and agile figure, her magnificent hair, her clothes, but also the majestic demeanour which she had adopted in the meantime.

During this period, and only then, did she allow portraits of herself to be made. She felt herself under pressure to ensure that her youthful beauty remained in people's memory. As soon as she noticed the first signs of ageing she withdrew from the public eye. As she reached middle-age she hardly allowed any more portraits to be made of herself. She began to hide her face behind what became inevitable fans when she appeared in public. Artists who had been commissioned to paint her portrait had to resort to the earlier pictures of her. So it is almost impossible to know what she really looked like later on in life (see pages 114 and 115 for a comparison).

Sisi at twenty-six years old.

A breathtaking appearance in a fur-trimmed overcoat.

Elisabeth has grown more self-confident and this can be seen in her demeanour.

We hardly ever see Sisi looking so relaxed,
she is almost smirking with pleasure.

An elaborate dress like this one could, when necessary, be sewn by thirty dress-makers in only two days.

The invoice document at the top of the page reads:

Fol.

Wien. 1. Albrechtsplatz 3. 6. Juli 1894.

Wilhelm Jungmann & Neffe

k. u. k. Hoflieferanten

Kammer
Ihrer Majestät Kaiserin Elisabeth.

Zahlbar in Wien.

1894

Schwarze Serge Toilette
schwarzer uni Tongis Blouse   ƒ 270
Schwarze Serge Mantille   ƒ 130   ƒ 400

Reclamationen binnen 14 Tagen.

325

Wien, am 12. 9. 1894

Empress Elisabeth and aristocratic ladies of the time favoured the quality of fabric to be found at Wilhelm Jungmann & Neffe's, purveyors of cloth by Imperial appointment. This is an original invoice made out to Elisabeth for 6th July 1894.

The historic interior of the shop, which dates back to the year 1881, has remained unaltered. Especially notable is the painting on the ceiling by Franz Lefler (1831–1898).

*…and magnificent hair. Here Sisi is to be seen
wearing her most famous hairstyle: Her floor-
length chestnut brown hair was plaited into several
strands and then wound around her head like a
diadem with a veil.*

Sisi dressed to emphasise her waist…

Most portraits of the Empress show her looking either serious or melancholy, which may be seen as a reflection of her state-of-mind.

We never see the real Empress smiling as radiantly as Romy Schneider here. She played the starring role in the three famous 'Sissy' films made in the fifties. These films still help shape the gushingly romantic image we have of Elisabeth today.

Sisi collected these famed and valuable stars for her hair, eventually owning twenty-seven of them. She wore them as a diadem, or individually scattered in her hair. Reproductions manufactured into various pieces of jewellery, are available in the shops of the Sisi Museum in the Hofburg and at Schönbrunn Palace.

The official portrait of three painted by Franz Xaver Winterhalter. Sisi made an exception for this artist by actually posing live for him. Franz Joseph wrote to his mother: 'The pictures he has painted of Sisi have turned out very charming and are the first portraits which actually show a true likeness'.

The Empress also allowed Franz Xaver Winterhalter to paint two portraits of her which were considered very familiar for the time, her hair was down (here and right). This was Franz Joseph's favourite picture, he had it put up in his study at Schönbrunn.

Sisi's hair was later to go right down to her ankles. To support the weight and soothe her headaches, it sometimes had to be strung-up on a cord above the Empress as she sat.

In the 1860s, at the
height of her beauty,
Sisi often had her
portrait painted.
Until then she
preferred wearing
white or light
colours. As she was
approaching her
thirtieth birthday the
official portraits
became fewer and her
clothes darker. She
soon refused to have
herself photographed
or her portrait
painted for the public
altogether.

At this time she was starting to favour black clothes, and following Rudolf's death she only ever wore mourning. Here is one of the later photographs, taken as she was in her early thirties.

ELISABETH'S LOVE OF HUNGARY

The Empress only once committed herself to pursuing a political issue with real vehemence. This was the *Ausgleich* — Compromise — with Hungary. She adored the Hungarian temperament, the people's love of freedom and their pride. To gain a better understanding of the mentality and culture there, she even learned to speak the difficult Hungarian language perfectly. She took it on herself to reconcile the Hungarian people with her husband.

At the heart of the problem was Franz Joseph's coronation, which the Hungarians insisted upon. As this was linked to the re-ratification of the Hungarian constitution, which means the endorsement of ancient laws guaranteeing them a special position within the monarchy. Franz Joseph and his mother neither wanted to restrict the authority of the monarchy, nor to accept the idea that the God-given right of the monarch's absolute power might be subjected to the will of the people. Sophie and Franz Joseph could not forgive the Hungarians for their participation in the revolution of 1848 and thought that they should be kept under control by the use of increased military force. They did not want to believe in any kind of Compromise. Despite this Sisi brought one about.

A deep fondness developed between the Empress and the leader of the pro-Hungarian movement, Count Gyula Andrássy, based on mutual personal fascination and a shared love of Hungary. It lasted until Andrássy's death in 1890. Despite many rumours to the contrary, their friendship always remainet a platonic one.

Even before the Compromise, Elisabeth often wore traditional Hungarian costume to demonstrate her love for the land.

ÉLJEN ERZSÉBET – QUEEN OF HUNGARY

The Viennese Court led by Archduchess Sophie was still against the pro-Hungarian movement. Elisabeth had learned to use her influence on the Emperor in the meantime, though. She had gone beyond the stage of begging for love and understanding, seeking a substitute for a lack of personal happiness in the realisation of her own aims and wishes instead. She won her cause at the start of 1867: The Compromise was ratified and Hungary's old constitution was restored. Out of the Austrian Empire emerged the Dual Monarchy of Austria and Hungary.

There was nothing left to prevent a coronation. It was held on 6th June 1867 at St. Matthew's in Budapest, and represented one of the most moving climaxes of her life. Franz Liszt had composed his Coronation Mass especially for the occasion and it was performed during the service. The magnificent celebrations lasted for four days and the royal couple was presented with Gödöllö Palace by the Hungarian people. It became one of Elisabeth's favourite residences in the years to come.

The official portrait showing the newly crowned Queen of Hungary.

The magnificent event was held at St. Matthew's in Budapest

According to Hungarian tradition, at the coronation the crown was placed upon the king's head and then held over the new queen's right shoulder. Here the Archbishop of Hungary is passing the crown to Gyula Andrássy, the prime minister, for this ceremony.

Elisabeth in her coronation dress.

Elisabeth and the family in front of their beloved Gödöllö Palace in Hungary.

Today the palace is open to the public.

The beautiful facade to the reputed firm J. & L. Lobmeyr has been carefully restored in the style of Franz Joseph's time.

The Gödöllö Service with a Chinese style pattern was designed by Herend, the Hungarian porcelain manufacturers, specially for the Empress. It was, as the name suggests, used in her favourite residence. The same service is still on sale to this day at J. & L. Lobmeyr in Vienna and Salzburg, suppliers of fine porcelain and glassware, formerly purveyors to the Imperial Court by appointment.

ELISABETH'S "ONLY CHILD" – MARIE VALERIE

Elisabeth and Franz Joseph grew completely estranged from one another over the years. She did not see this as a failing as she was not a very sensuous woman. Their married life was a matter of duty and as far as children were concerned, she felt she had done what had been expected of her.

Nevertheless, her pleasure at the compromise with Hungary did revive her relationship with Franz Joseph for a while and she made an exception to her resolve not to become pregnant again. Just a year after the coronation she gave birth to a little girl, Marie Valerie, in Budapest. At the Viennese Court she was spitefully dubbed the 'Hungarian child'. Sisi saw her as her 'only child' as it was the only one that she was finally allowed to always have around her and whom she could watch growing-up. She took Marie Valerie everywhere she went and enjoyed being a mother with all her heart: 'Now I know what happiness a child means — now I have shown the courage to bestow her with my love and keep her by me'.

One of the ways she expressed her love for her daughter was by supporting her so that she could avoid having to make a marriage of convenience, giving her time to find a husband for herself. Marie Valerie's choice fell on Archduke Franz Salvator. After waiting two and a half years to be sure, as her mother had advised her to, she married him in 1890. Elisabeth felt profound anguish at the loss of her daughter to a man.

Marie Valerie (1868-1925), the youngest daughter, bore the strongest resemblance to Elisabeth. With her, Elisabeth was at last able to savour the pleasures of motherhood.

Marie Valerie was given time to be sure that she had met the right man before she married him. She chose Archduke Franz Salvator.

Marie Valerie and Franz Salvator had nine children. Here they are to be seen with the first three on a visit to their grandparents, the Emperor and Empress.

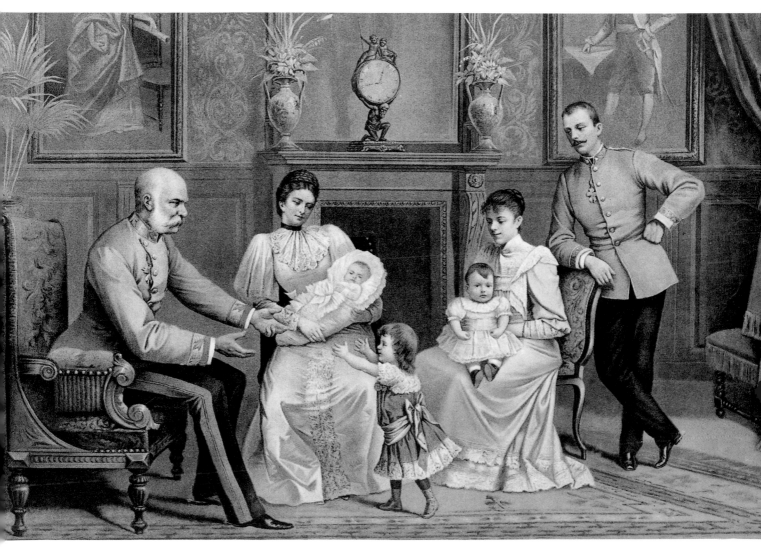

ELISABETH'S TRUE PASSIONS RIDING...

Elisabeth's undisguised love of Hungary only deepened the cleft between the Viennese Court and herself still further. Sophie's influence was weakening. In particular the execution of her second son, Emperor Maximilian of Mexico, had broken her iron will and she spent the last five years of her life in a state of deep reclusion. Elisabeth would have been able to become the most powerful woman in the empire as at the time she was able to exert great influence on her husband. But she was no longer interested in that anymore. The tough times and disappointments of her first years of marriage had hardened her, she had become increasingly shy of public appearances, more reserved, more lonely within and less approachable. She travelled to Hungary frequently as she felt less constrained there than in Vienna, she also sought the company of her own family circle in Bavaria.

A time began which was almost solely dedicated to riding and she spent long periods of months in England, France and Ireland. This dangerous sport, perilous because she pursued it with such an obsession, was to almost entirely dominate her life for about a decade. She owned the most thoroughbred of horses and trained with a grim determination, often to the point of complete exhaustion. This helped to make her one of the best horsewomen of her time. She did not just participate in steeplechases, hunting and dressage events, she could also drive a carriage and even practised circus tricks with horses. To this end, she had a circus rink erected at Gödöllö.

Sisi dressed for riding. She even had herself stitched into these clothes. Before her exhausting rides she drank a bowl of strong broth and two glasses of wine for fortification.

The Empress was a stunning looking woman even when she was out riding. Her niece Marie Wallersee described her as follows: 'Elisabeth looked enchanting even on horseback. Her hair lay in heavy plaits upon her head, above which she wore a top hat. Her costume looked as if it had been moulded to her; she wore high, laced boots with tiny spurs and had three pairs of gloves on, one on top of the other. The inevitable fan was always close at hand, slipped into her saddle.

Elisabeth could drive
carriages pulled by a
span of several
horses and had
mastered several
circus tricks to the
point of perfection.

Her fearlessness sometimes led to precarious situations. For instance, when her horse's hoof broke through a narrow bridge. A huntsman saved the Empress from falling into the raging alpine river below.

Elisabeth was wearing this hat when she fell and nearly killed herself in Sassetôt (Normandy) on 11th September 1875.

LITERATURE
AND FOREIGN LANGUAGES

She had never been interested in the sort of shallow conversation which provided the focus of Court gossip or social functions, and she avoided it. Paradoxically her silence on such occasions gave her the reputation of not being very intelligent. In reality she was a very well-read and highly educated woman. 'If the day were only once so long; I cannot learn and read as much as I would wish'. She was a great admirer of Heinrich Heine, she loved Shakespeare and was an avid reader of the works of writers and poets ranging from Homer to Goethe. She was highly versed in history, mythology and philosophy, she spoke fluent English, French and Hungarian, and in the late 1880s she began learning ancient and modern Greek. At Court nobody spoke of anything beyond theatre gossip and who had met whom in the Prater (a park), and even Franz Joseph found what he saw as the abstract musings of his wife incomprehensible, even somewhat suspicious. She had always been a very caring person but as a result of her studies, her basic attitude became more profound. She developed into an individual with liberal democratic leanings and a keen sense of general awareness. She felt nothing but disdain for the arrogant and conceited aristocracy, feelings which she expressed in writing. She also wrote poetry, and with this she hoped to provide posterity with an insight into her world, her political and personal opinions as well as the problems she had to face. About ten years before her death, she deposited her complete poems, which encompass about 600 printed pages, in Switzerland with the instructions to publish them sixty years later. They were made available to us, 'the souls of the future', in the fifties.

The writing set which Sisi used, it is made of gold-plated silver and lapis lazuli.

Words To Souls Of The Future (excerpt)

I wander lonely before me on this planet earth
All yearning long since gone, and life;
To share my innermost is no companion.
There never was a soul who understood.

I flee the world, its pleasures too,
And its people are distant to me now;
Their joys are foreign and their distress;
I wander lonely as if upon a star.

And my soul, heavy to burst,
Mute sensuality is not enough.
What it needs is found in song
And this I am burying in my book.

This will keep you faithfully into age
From souls who understand you not in this life;
Till one day, following lengthy years of change,
These songs, blooming, do revive.

TRAVELLING

'The destinations are only attractive in so far as the journey to them lies between...' Elisabeth's restlessness, which she did not just show in her sporting activities, but even when she was doing the most mundane things, was also the motivation behind her time-consuming and lengthy travels. She usually travelled under a pseudonym to avoid any public receptions and representational duties.

To make it more attractive for her to stay close to the Court, while still satisfying her yearning for privacy, Franz Joseph had the so-called Hermes Villa built in the middle of an expanse of shooting grounds, the Lainzer Tiergarten to the west of Vienna.

For her part, though, she was far more involved in the progress of the construction of her Villa "Achilleion" on the Greek island of Corfu. However she could never bear to remain in either of the two places for more than a couple of days at once. She regularly crossed the Mediterranean on one of her yachts, the Miramare or the Greif, or took a specially adapted train right across Europe to England, Ireland, Gödöllö, Biarritz, Bad Kissingen, Holland, Corfu, the Côte d'Azur, Dresden, Algeria, Naples, Switzerland, Lisbon, Barcelona, Corsica, Greece or Milan…

When Franz Joseph gave this travelling service to Sisi on their engagement he did not know what a fatal significance it would come to have.

Elisabeth named her villa on Corfu Achilleion
after her favourite hero, Achilles.

The vast expanse of woodland and meadows used for hunting surrounding the Hermes Villa, named after the Greek God of the same name, has been preserved to this day. Elisabeth neither stayed here for very long, nor very often.

The magnificent bedroom in the Hermes Villa. The painter Gustav Klimt, at the time almost unknown, decorated the walls with scenes from Shakespeare's 'A Midsummer Night's Dream'.

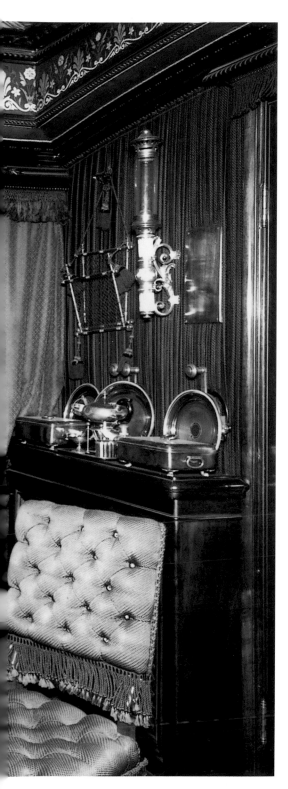

For her travels within Europe Elisabeth took a specially adapted train. These pictures show her salon carriage (left) and her sleeping quarters (right).

SHOPPING

One of Elisabeth's weaknesses was for shopping. She was especially fastidious when it came to things destined for her own personal use, which had to comply to the highest standards. She was particularly careful to make sure that only products of the very best quality were obtained for her clothing and personal hygiene as well as in what she ate. This helped earn her a reputation as an eccentric.

Quite a few old established shops or firms are allowed to bear the imperial arms with the inscription 'K.u.K.' with pride, to show that they used to supply the Imperial Court at the time of the monarchy. The letters stand for 'Kaiserlich und Königlich' — meaning that they were purveyors to the Court by Royal and Imperial appointment. This honour was only seldom granted, and applicants were many: So would-be appointees had not just to offer excellent goods or the best service, they also had to be model citizens, have integrity and be free of debts. Although occasionally members of the Imperial Family also awarded the title of Purveyor to the Court to tradesmen of their own accord if they were particularly pleased with what they offered. Empress Elisabeth did this on at least two occasions. Court officials ensured that the standards of quality were maintained and if there were any complaints, the title could be withdrawn. So the firms bearing the K.u.K. inscription guarantee the first class quality for their wares once demanded by the Imperial Court.

A few examples of former purveyors to the Imperial Court by appointment. Now, as then, they aim to continue to fulfil the high standards formerly demanded of them by Elisabeth and the rest of the courtiers.

interior design

Showroom:
BACKHAUSEN INTERIOR DESIGN GmbH
Schwarzenbergstr.10, 1010 WIEN (Vienna) ÖSTERREICH (Austria)
Tel: +43-1-51404-0, Fax: +43-1-51404-62
e-mail: vienna@backhausen.com
www.backhausen.com

Rahmen - Spiegel
A-1010 Wien, Michaelerplatz 6
Telefon 0043-1-533 10 49, Fax 0043-1-535 49 60
www.buehlmayer.at

KAIS. u. KÖNIGL.
HOF-u. KAMMERLIEFERANTEN
GEGRÜNDET 1866.

Wilhelm Jungmann & Neffe

SEIDEN-u. WOLLSTOFFE

A-1010 Wien, Albertinaplatz 3
Telefon 0043-1-512 18 75, Fax 0043-1-512 14 65

LOBMEYR®

1 8 2 3

Kärntnerstraße 26, A-1015 Wien
Tel.: +43-1-512 05 08, Fax: +43-1-512 05 08 85
Filiale: Schwarzstraße 20, A-5020 Salzburg
e-mail: lobmeyr@compuserve.com

THE BURDEN OF THE CROWN

One of the most unbearable experiences for Elisabeth was, from her first day in Vienna onwards, being stared at by thousands of pairs of eyes and being treated as public property. She was just as unable and unwilling to accustom herself to the stiffness of court ceremonial, which she regarded as futile. She also took no pleasure whatsoever in superficial conversation and hollow clichés. All this led to an almost overwhelming abhorrence of all forms of public appearance. Wherever she could she avoided these occasions, either by a complete absence from Vienna or with a row of thin excuses.

She could not bear to take on any form of representational duties unless these were entirely unavoidable. And she showed her discomfort whenever she had to go 'in full tackle', as she referred to her appearances in formal attire, to be exposed to everybody's scrutiny and at the focus of attention. For instance, at her sixteen-year old daughter Gisela's wedding. At the time Sisi was thirty-five years old and not particularly enthusiastic at the prospect of becoming a grandmother in the near future. She was only seldom to be seen at the 1873 World Exhibition in Vienna and, in the same year, appeared on only two days to participate in the 25th Jubilee of the Emperor's reign. The magnificent convoy on the occasion of the Emperor and Empress' Silver Wedding, which was organised by the famous painter Hans Makart, did not thrill her at all: 'It's already enough to have been married for twenty-five years without also having to celebrate the fact'.

The Main Gallery at Schönbrunn was lit by 1,000 candles at gala dinners, the table was 30 metres long.

Even family diners, held on magnificently laid banqueting tables in the palace like the one shown here, were a strain for Elisabeth.

The Emperor and Empress' Silver Wedding in 1879. Elisabeth did not feel like celebrating twenty-five years of a marriage which had been the source of such grief to her.

Elisabeth bought a brooch like the one above at the 1873 World Exhibition. Shown below is a detail of the bracelet Franz Joseph gave her on their 25th Wedding Anniversary.

One of the Empress' favourite pastimes was to get away from the Court with all its formality and protocol and do normal things in anonymity, like going on a shopping spree.

She often enjoyed popping into the patisseries when she was out on one of these trips. Despite her diet, she had phases of not being able to resist sweets and often ate astonishing quantities in a single sitting.

She was particularly fond of candied violets. These are produced according to an old, traditional process and sold at the former K.u.K. purveyors to the Court, Gerstner.

Elisabeth tried to shield herself from
inquisitive glances by using a fan or a parasol.

ELISABETH AS A MATCHMAKER FOR FRANZ JOSEPH

The reasons why Empress Elisabeth, of all people, should have played matchmaker for her husband will never really be known. Did she take pity on her ageing husband, or was her conscience plaguing her as she left him alone so often? Or did she want to gain more independence from him? In any case, the fact is that she established the contact between the Emperor and the highly acclaimed actress, Katherina Schratt, and intervened to nurture the alliance between the two of them. She probably had no idea that Franz Joseph had been having an affair with a young woman called Anna Nahowski since 1875, and that this coincided with his relationship with Katherina Schratt for four years before he put an end to the affair.

The Emperor was very much in love with the actress, who was twenty-three years younger than himself. Though how far this romance actually went cannot be ascertained with any certainty. In any case, 'the lady friend' remained the emperor's confidant for over thirty years. It is possible that they entered into a secret marriage following the death of both of their spouses. Documents which might have delivered proof of this were lost in 1945 when St. Stephan's Cathedral caught fire.

Franz Joseph had an affair with Anna Nahowski lasting fourteen years. They met in the park of the palace or at Anna's house on Maxingstrasse, which runs along the palace wall. Incidentally, this was not far away from the villa Katherina Schratt lived in.

Anna's daughter Helene was Franz Joseph's child. Helene later married the well-known composer Alban Berg.

The actress Katherina Schratt remained the 'lady friend' to the Emperor for three decades. Elisabeth was already well beyond any feelings of jealousy and had even brought the two of them together.

Franz Joseph loved the strolls and conversations with Mrs. Schratt, who was a kindly and down-to-earth woman.

THE MAYERLING TRAGEDY

One particular twist of fate robbed Elisabeth of the last of her ability to enjoy life: On 30th January 1889 her only son, Crown Prince Rudolf, took his own life taking his seventeen-year old lover, Baroness Mary Vetsera, with him. The tragedy occurred at Rudolf's hunting lodge, Mayerling, in the south of the Vienna Woods and came completely unexpectedly to everybody, even the closest members of the family. Nobody knew of the extent of the problems facing the heir to the throne, let alone could have guessed that he would commit suicide. Rudolf was survived by his wife, the former Belgian princess Stephanie, and a daughter, the little Archduchess Elisabeth.

For the rest of her life, the Empress was a broken woman. She never wore anything but mourning until the day of her death, nine years later, and her restlessness only increased.

Mary Vetsera shortly before her tragic demise. For Rudolf she was only one of many lovers. She was, in contrast to him though, hopelessly in love with the Crown Prince and so she was prepared to join him in death. To avoid publicity, she was buried at night in the utmost of secrecy and without rites in the nearby cemetery at Heiligenkreuz.

The thirty-one year old Crown Prince Rudolf lying in state. The bandage on his head is to hide the wound left where he shot himself.

His young widow Stephanie with their only child, the Archduchess Elisabeth. Following the end of the monarchy, she joined the Social Democratic Movement and went down in history as the Red Archduchess.

Rudolf being laid to rest in the Imperial Crypt under the Capuchian church in Vienna. The doctor who carried out the autopsy attested that Rudolf had not been responsible for his actions at the time of his suicide. This meant that he could be buried on hallowed ground.

Elisabeth wearing mourning at the age of fifty-seven. As she no longer posed for official portraits, artists had to use pictures of the young Empress to paint her portrait from. This is how Armin Horowitz completed this portrait, too.

Even at the millennial celebrations for her beloved Hungary in 1896, she wore a black noble costume and appeared apathetic and infinitely sad amidst the solemn ceremony.

A snapshot from the last years of the Empress' life, taken during a stay in Territet, Switzerland.

A VIOLENT DEATH IN GENEVA

On 10th September 1898 in Geneva, the Italian anarchist Luigi Lucheni put an end to Elisabeth's life. He stabbed a carpenter's file into her heart as she was on her way to board a ship. For a little while the situation did not look too serious, the stab-wound was so small that no-one noticed it and everybody involved thought that she had just been hit with a bare fist. The Empress stood up and went on board the ship. It was only there that she collapsed and died. The whole thing happened only a few hundred metres away from the Beau-Rivage Hotel where she had spent the night.

Her violent death has one particularly tragic element: Lucheni's real target had been the Prince of Orléans, as a representative of the aristocracy he so hated. However the Prince had cancelled his planned trip to Geneva and in the newspaper it had stated that the Empress of Austria was there, even though she was travelling incognito under the pseudonym of the Countess of Hohenembs. As the assailant was not interested in any one person in particular, but in striking back at the aristocracy in general, he chose the Empress to be his victim.

She was laid to rest in the Capuchian Crypt (Kapuzinergruft), the traditional burial place for members of the Imperial Family. Her coffin lies alongside those of her son and her husband.

A portrait of the dead Empress by the sculptor Robert Weigl. A year after her murder, the Court ordered this elegant frame for a photograph of the piece from the frame makers and guilders by Imperial appointment, C. Bühlmayer, a firm which still exists to this day and has its premises in Michaelerdurchgang in the centre of Vienna.

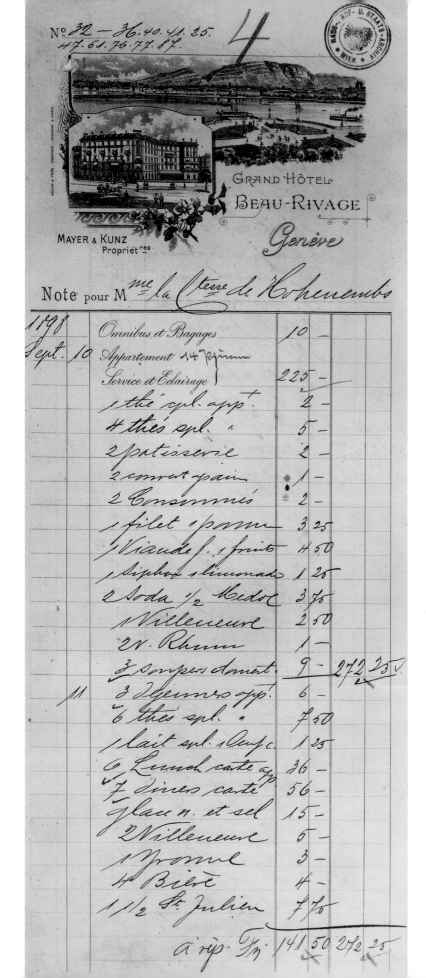

The bill for lunch from the Beau-Rivage Hotel in Geneva. It is made out to Empress Elisabeth under her pseudonym the Countess of Hohenembs, on the day of her murder.

The place where Luigi Lucheni stabbed the Empress in the heart with a file is to be seen to the right at the bottom of the picture.

The murderer is taken away, obviously pleased with himself. He has just struck a successful blow against the establishment. It does not really matter to him whom he has actually killed. He was sentenced to lifelong imprisonment and hanged himself in his cell after eleven years in jail.

The dress Elisabeth was wearing at the time of her murder. The stab-wound next to her heart is clearly visible.

The Empress' state procession to Vienna begins. Here, her coffin is being carried out of the Beau-Rivage Hotel.

*Lying in state at the railway
station in Geneva.*

*Elisabeth lying in state at the
Hofburg palace chapel in Vienna.*

This hearse was pulled by eight black horses and was not just used for Empress Elisabeth and Emperor Franz Joseph as well as Crown Prince Rudolf, it was also used to take Zita, the last Empress of Austria, to her final resting place in the Capuchian Crypt.

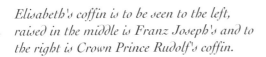

*Elisabeth's coffin is to be seen to the left,
raised in the middle is Franz Joseph's and to
the right is Crown Prince Rudolf's coffin.*

*A marble statue of the Empress in the
Volksgarten in Vienna. It was unveiled in
1907 in the presence of the seventy-seven
year old Emperor*

Here are just a few suggestions for those interested in retracing Sisi's footsteps and learning more about her, or simply finding a souvenir to take home.

Schönbrunn Palace: The state rooms of this former imperial summer residence bear witness not only to the grandeur of receptions, ceremonies and balls once held by the Habsburgs. They also grant insight into the private quarters and everyday life of Elisabeth and Franz Joseph.

Special tours billed as "Experience Schönbrunn" are yet another attraction. Dressed up in period costume, children and youngsters can experience what life must have been like for imperial offspring, learning the language of the fan and much more besides. The new baroque maze is another source of fascination for young and old alike.

Schönbrunn boasts a number of well-assorted shops stocking a wealth of additional reading material on Elisabeth, as well as fine giftware. They are to be found:

- at the end of the "Imperial" and "Grand" tours,
- at the tobacconists (Tabak-Trafik) to the left of the main entrance

Hofburg: After a tour through the Imperial Silver Collection, the Sisi Museum awaits you. Here the "myth of Sisi" is staged apart from all the common clichés. In addition to famous portraits and a life size statue, which is made to her original measurements, the museum shows a multitude of personal objects such as fans, pieces of jewellery and dresses that belonged to the empress, as well as venturing forth with a quite critical view of her. Continuing on you will reach the imperial apartments, the historical and authentic living quarters of Emperor Franz Joseph and Empress Elisabeth. In the dressing and gymnastic room you can see to this day the wall bars and rings that were used by the athletic empress, and in the bathroom, Elisabeth's bathtub.

A large selection of beautiful souvenirs are on sale at the shops in the entrance area by the Imperial Silver Collection and at the end of the tour of the imperial apartments.

Imperial Furniture Collection: Among the many items used by the imperial household over the centuries, you can view the scales Elisabeth weighed herself with every day, Crown Prince Rudolf's cradle and the furnishings from Emperor Franz Joseph's study.

Hermesvilla: A walk through the wonderful Lainz Game Reserve takes you to this commemorative site. Every year, the villa is used for special exhibitions on Empress Elisabeth and related subjects.

The emperor's villa in Bad Ischl: Emperor Franz Josef I resided here with his wife Elisabeth during the summer months. Even today you can still experience the personal ambiance of the emperor in unchanged conditions. Open from: May 1 – mid - October (10 a.m. - 4.45 p.m.).

Gödöllö Palace: Located some 30 km east of Budapest, Gödöllö Palace was a place where Sisi felt happy and free. After World War II the building fell into a state of decay. But it has now been restored to its former splendour and opened its doors to the public again in 1996. The large stateroom, the restored royal apartments and the Elisabeth commemorative exhibition are now permanent attractions. Various cultural events, including concerts, theatre productions, markets and exhibitions, are hosted throughout the year. The rooms and gardens may also be hired for business or private functions.

Illustration Credits:

Austrian National Library:
7, 9, 20, 24, 25, 37, 39, 43, 45 right, 53 top, 55, 60, 61, 62, 64, 65, 66 bottom, 71, 73, 76, 78/79, 83 bottom, 84, 85, 88 top, 88 bottom, 89 top, 90, 96, 97, 104, 105, 107 right, 109, 113, 114, 115 both, 117, 118, 120 right, 121, 122, 123

Wien Museum:
8 bottom, 11, 14, 18, 22, 31 top, 33, 34, 35, 36, 40, 41, 56, 58/59, 66 top, 70, 80 top, 82, 83 top, 86, 95, 102 right, 106, 108, 110, 111, 112 top, 112 bottom, 119

Museum of Fine Arts, Vienna:
13, 15, 17, 28, 31 bottom, 57, 67 left, 69, 124 bottom

Archive for Art and History, Berlin:
32

Munich Stadtmuseum:
8 top

Munich Stadtmuseum, photographic department:
45 left

Hungarian National Museum, Budapest:
51 top, 51 bottom, 89 bottom, 120 left

The Fürst Thurn und Taxis Collection:
68

Kaiservilla Besichtigungsbetriebsges.m.b.H.
12

Austrian Tourist Board/photo by Trumler:
16, 19, 26 bottom, 29, 75, 101 top

Austrian Tourist Board/photo by Simoner:
23

Austrian Tourist Board/photo by Kalmar:
26 top

Austrian Tourist Board/photo by Markowitsch:
94

Austrian Tourist Board/photo by Wiesenhofer:
100

Austrian Tourist Board/photo by Muhr:
124 top

Austrian Tourist Board/photo by Haider:
125

Schloss Schönbrunn Kultur and Bietriebsgesellschaft:
27

SSKB/photo by J. Wagner:
47, 50 top, 54, 101 bottom

SSKB/photo by M. Haller:
49, 52

SSKB/photo by Haiden u. Baumann:
91, 92,

The Alban Berg Foundation:
107 left

The Hungarian Tourist Board:
72, 74, 77

The Greek Central Office for Tourism:
93

Gödöllö Palace administration:
80 bottom

Museums Collection:
44, 102 top left, 102 bottom left

Julius Meinl:
98, 103 top

Lobmeyr:
81 top, 81 bottom

Backhausen:
50 bottom

Jungmann & Neffe:
63 top, 63 bottom

Gerstner:
103 middle, 103 bottom

C. Bühlmeyer:
116

private collection, Germany:
53 bottom

Zentrum für Aussergewöhnliche Museen (ZAM), Munich:
6

Treasure chamber of Maria Taferl
21

Schloss Schönbrunn Kultur- und Betriebsges.m.b.H.
67 right

Renate Hofbauer
26 bottom

acknowledgement:
Translation of the poetry on page 23: Brigitte Hamann, 1997, Elisabeth. *The Reluctant Empress.* Berlin: Ullstein Verlag